The Wooden Horse of Troy

re-told by
Philip Page

D1434572

Published in association with
The Basic Skills Agency

Hodder & Stoughton

A MEMBER OF THE HO

Acknowledgements
Cover: Doug Lewis
Illustrations: Philip Page

Orders; please contact Bookpoint Ltd, 39 Milton Park, Abingdon, Oxon OX14 4TD. Telephone: (44) 01235 400414, Fax: (44) 01235 400454. Lines are open from 9.00–6.00, Monday to Saturday, with a 24 hour message answering service. Email address: orders@bookpoint.co.uk

British Library Cataloguing in Publication Data
A catalogue record for this title is available from the British Library

ISBN 0 340 77679 X

First published 2000
Impression number 10 9 8 7 6 5 4 3 2 1
Year   2005 2004 2003 2002 2001 2000

Copyright © 2000 Philip Page

Typeset by GreenGate Publishing Services, Tonbridge, Kent.
Printed in Great Britain for Hodder and Stoughton Educational, a division of Hodder Headline Plc, 338 Euston Road, London NW1 3BH, by Atheneum Press, Gateshead, Tyne & Wear

The Wooden Horse of Troy

Contents

How to say the names

Priam (Pry-am) – King of Troy, father of Hector and Paris.

Hera (Here-rah) – Queen of the gods.

Athene (Ath-eeny) – goddess of wisdom and war.

Aphrodite (Aafro-dy-tee) – goddess of love.

Menelaus (Men-ee-lay-uss) – King of Sparta and Helen's husband before she ran off with Paris.

Agamemnon (Agga-mem-non) – a powerful Greek king and brother of Menelaus.

Achilles (Ack-ill-ees) – bravest warrior in all Greece.

Odysseus (Oh-diss-ee-uss) – a Greek king who was warned not to go to Troy.

Prylis (Pry-liss) – a Greek warrior who thought of the idea of the Wooden Horse.

1

The Judgement of Paris

Long ago the Greeks believed in many gods
and goddesses.
They lived on Mount Olympus.
Three of these goddesses had a quarrel.
They could not agree which of them
was the most beautiful.

They appeared one day before a young human.
His name was Paris.
His father was King Priam of Troy.

'You must judge which of us is the most
beautiful,' they told Paris.
'Give this golden apple to the one you choose.'

Paris was afraid.
He knew he would upset the two
he did not choose.
He also knew that he had to do what they said.
You did not disobey a god or goddess!

The first goddess was called Hera.
She was the queen of the gods.
'If you choose me,' she said,
'I will make you rich and powerful.'

The second goddess was called Athene.
She was the goddess of wisdom and war.
'If you choose me,' she said,
'I will make you brave and wise.'

The third goddess was called Aphrodite.
She was the goddess of love.
'Choose me,' she said, 'and the most
beautiful woman in the world
will fall in love with you.'

It did not take long for Paris
to make up his mind.
He gave the golden apple to Aphrodite.

2

Paris and Helen

Paris knew who the most beautiful woman
in the world was.
Everybody in the Greek world knew!
Her name was Helen,
but she was already married.
Her husband was King Menelaus of Sparta.

Paris wondered if the goddess
had told him the truth.
He soon got the chance to find out.
His father, King Priam,
sent him to visit Sparta.

Menelaus welcomed Paris.
He gave a feast in his honour.
It lasted for nine days and nights.

Helen was at the feast.
Paris had never seen anybody so lovely.
He fell in love with her
as soon as he saw her.
But would she fall in love with him?

At the end of the nine days and nights,
Menelaus had to go on a journey.
He left Helen behind.

Paris told her that he loved her.
He asked her to leave Menelaus
and return with him to Troy.
Helen agreed and they sailed away
the next day.

When Menelaus came back
he found out what had happened.
He was furious!
He thought that Paris had kidnapped his wife.
He did not know about Aphrodite's promise.
He did not know that Helen had fallen in love
with Paris.

3

The Gathering of the Greeks

There were many kings in Greece in those days.
The most powerful was Agamemnon
of Mycenae.
Menelaus was his brother.

Menelaus went to see Agamemnon.
'Paris has kidnapped my wife,' he said.
'You must help me to get her back.'

'I will send a message to King Priam of Troy,'
said Agamemnon.
'If he does not send Helen back,
we will take her back by force!'

Messengers were sent across the sea to Troy
in a fast ship.
Menelaus and Agamemnon did not like the news
they brought back.
They said that Helen did not want to come back.
They said that Priam had allowed her to stay.
They also said that Helen had married Paris!

Agamemnon gave orders for a great army
to gather.
He sent messages to all parts of Greece
for the kings to bring their soldiers.

From Pylus came old Nestor,
the wisest of kings.
From Crete came a hundred ships
filled with warriors.
From Salamis came Ajax,
one of the greatest fighters.
Young Achilles, in his golden armour, came too.
He was the bravest warrior in all Greece.
No part of his body could be harmed
by weapons, except for his heel.

Only one king remained – Odysseus of Ithaca.
A fortune-teller told him not to go to Troy.
If he did, it would be twenty years
before he saw his wife and home again.
He pretended to be mad
but the trick did not work.
He and his soldiers
joined the rest of the Greeks.

Achilles fell out with Agamemnon.
He said that he would not fight any more.
When the Trojans heard this they were happy.
Achilles was the best warrior
in the Greek army.

The best soldier in the Trojan army
was Hector, the son of King Priam.
Paris was his younger brother.
Hector led an attack on the Greeks.
In the fighting he killed Achilles's cousin.

Achilles looked at the dead body
of his cousin and wept with sadness and rage.
He swore that he would kill Hector.

He put on his gold armour and
took up his sword and shield.
In his chariot, he raced to the battle
to look for Hector.

The fight between Achilles and Hector
lasted for many hours.

At last Achilles killed Hector.
He tied his body to the back of his chariot
and dragged it three times
round the walls of Troy.

King Priam sent a messenger to beg
for Hector's body.
He wanted to bury his son.
Achilles was still angry.
'Give me his weight in gold and jewels,'
he said. 'Then you can have your son back.'

The Trojans buried Hector.
Achilles buried his cousin
and still the war went on.

Within a year, Achilles was dead.
He was killed by Paris who shot an arrow
into Achilles's heel.

Then Paris was killed.
Helen tried to escape from Troy
but she was caught.
She was forced to marry another Trojan.

6

The Wooden Horse

The war had now lasted for ten long years.
Many of the Greeks wondered
if they would ever see their homes again.
They began to think that they would never win.

One day, a Greek warrior called Prylis
went to see Agamemnon.
'We cannot get into Troy by force,' he said.
'We might be able to get in by a trick.'

'What is your plan?' Agamemnon asked.
Prylis told him.

The Greeks built a huge wooden horse.
Its belly was hollow.
It could hold about twenty men.

When it was finished Odysseus,
Menelaus and some other soldiers
hid inside the horse.
At night the Greeks pushed it up to
the walls of Troy.

In the morning the Greeks went to their ships
and pretended to sail away.
They did not go far –
just out of sight of Troy.

The Trojans came out to look at the horse.
They saw some words carved on it.

'The Greeks have given up,' one Trojan said.
'This carving says that the horse is a gift
to the goddess Athene,' said another.
'The Greeks want her to give them
a safe journey home,' said a third.

King Priam gave orders for the wooden horse
to be brought into the city.
Some Trojans were worried.
Priam's daughter told her father
that it was a trick.
'Beware of any gift from the Greeks,'
warned another Trojan.
Priam did not listen to them.

The wooden horse was too big to go through
the gates of the city.
They had to break down part of the walls
to get it through.
Then they rebuilt the gap.

That night the Trojans celebrated.
They feasted and drank.
They danced in the streets.
They thought that the war was over.
They thought that they had won.

That night there was a full moon.
By midnight all the Trojans were asleep.
Then Odysseus gave the order.

The Greeks inside the horse
opened a hidden trapdoor.
One by one they slid down a rope ladder.
Silently they killed the Trojan sentries.
Quietly they opened the great gates
of the city.

That same night the Greek ships had
come back.
The soldiers crept up to the walls of Troy.
When the gates were opened,
Agamemnon led his
army into the sleeping city.

7

The End of Troy

The Trojans were taken by surprise!
Their warriors were killed in their beds.
They did not have time to put on
their armour or to get their weapons.

The Greeks showed no mercy.
They ran through the city
killing every man they found.
They killed the women and children too.
They took all the gold and treasure.
Then they set fire to the houses.

The dark sky was turned red by the flames.
The full moon was the colour of blood.
Black smoke hid the stars.

Menelaus rushed to Priam's palace.
He wanted to find Helen.
He was going to kill her
because she had left him.
Then he saw how beautiful she still was.
He remembered how much he loved her.
He threw away his sword and took her
back to the ships.

King Priam was now an old man.
He tried to fight but a Greek soldier
killed him with a spear.
The Greeks cut off his head.
They took his body to Achilles's grave
and left it there to rot.

Agamemnon made Priam's daughter his slave.
He ordered the Greeks to tear down
the walls of Troy.

Troy had once been a beautiful city.
The Greeks left it a burning ruin.

8

The Greeks Return Home

The Greeks set sail for home.
Most of them had long and hard journeys.
Only Nestor had a safe journey
and lived a long and happy life.
Many died when storms sank their ships.

Strong winds blew Menelaus and Helen
to Crete and Egypt.
It was many years before they returned
to Sparta.

Agamemnon's wife was not pleased
to see him again.
She hadn't forgiven him for letting let their
daughter be put to death as a sacrifice.
She was angry that he had brought Priam's
daughter back with him.
On the day he got home she killed him
while he was having a bath.
Then she cut off the head of Priam's daughter.

What about Odysseus?
The fortune-teller had said he would not see
his home for twenty years.
He had fought at Troy for ten years.
Now he was forced to wander to many lands for
another ten years.

That is another story.